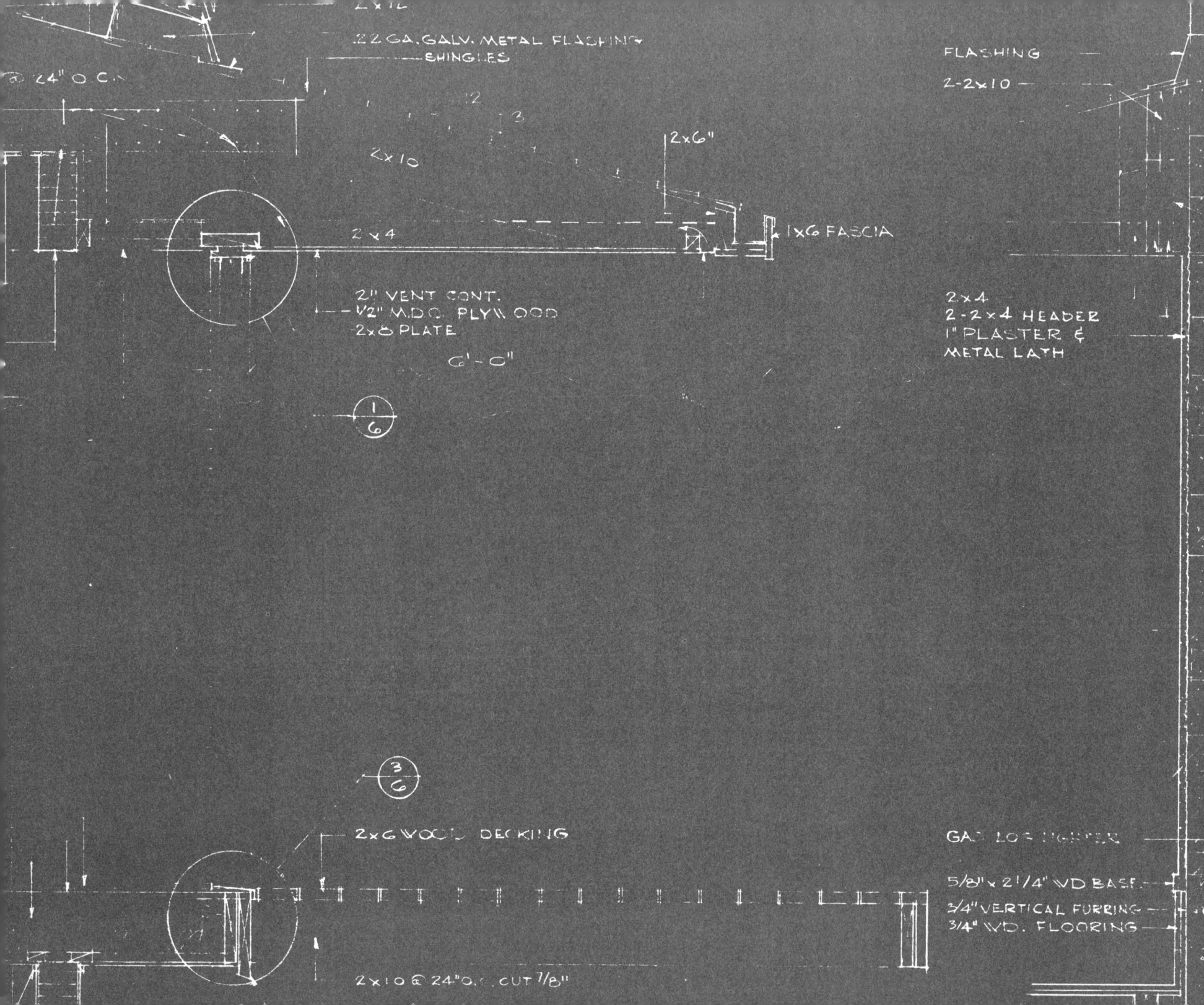

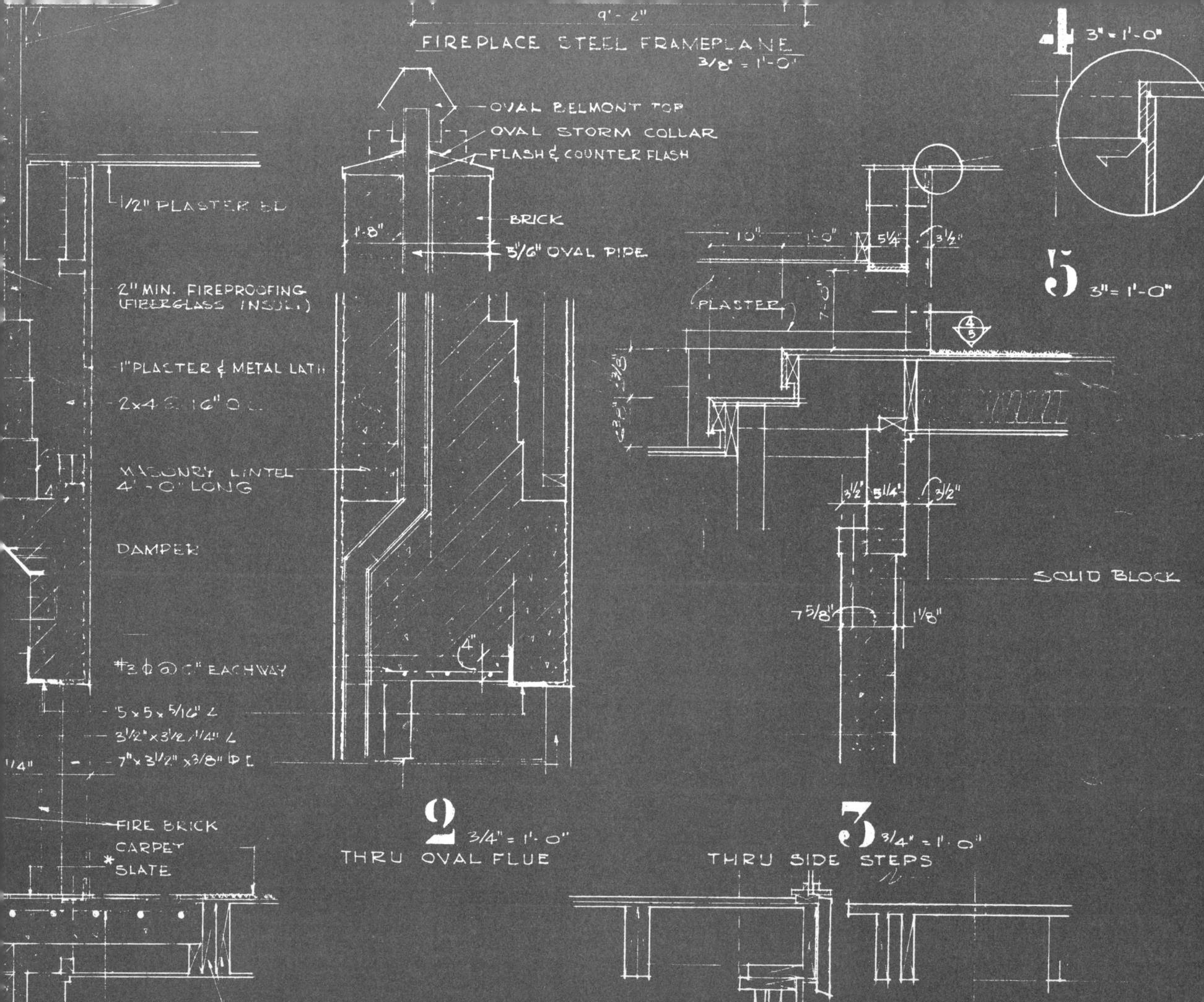

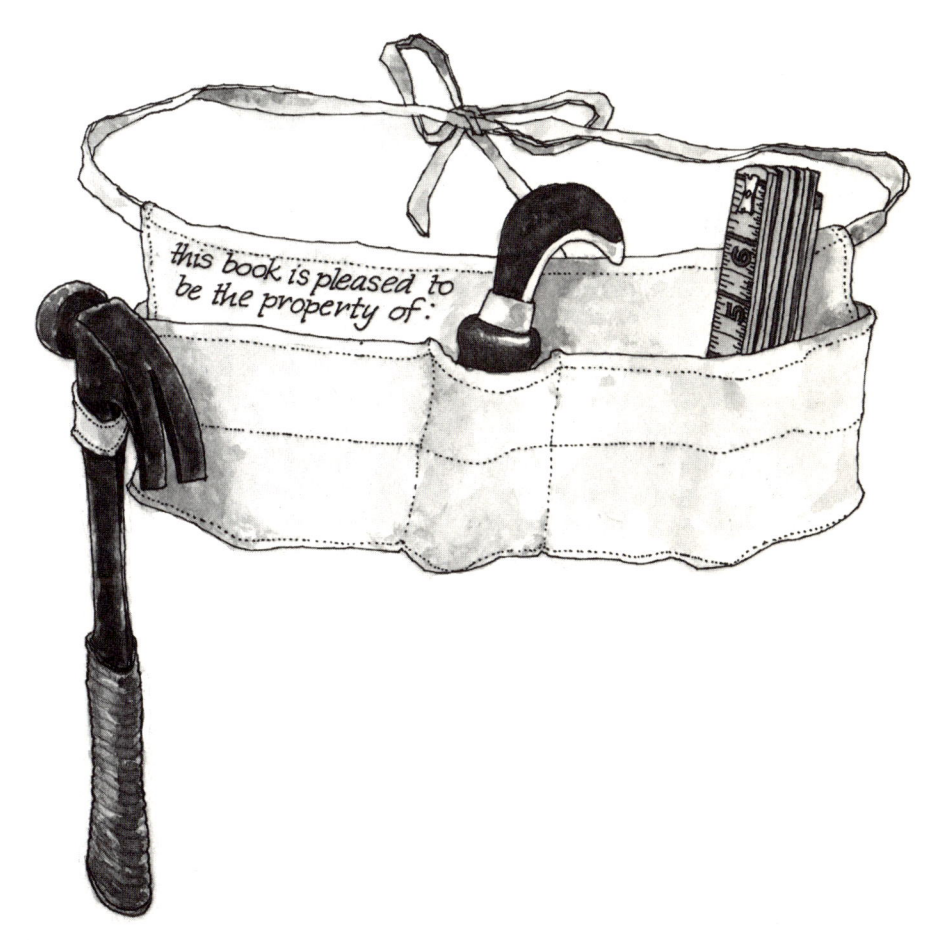

HOW A HOUSE HAPPENS

WALKER & COMPANY

THIS BOOK IS THE PROPERTY OF:

WRITTEN, DESIGNED AND ILLUSTRATED BY: JAN ADKINS

SPECIFICATIONS

2

LIBRARY OF CONGRESS CATALOGUE CARD NO.: 72-179616

TRADE EDITION: 0-8027-6093-7
REINFORCED ED: 0-8027-6094-5

RIGHTS: ALL RIGHTS ARE RESERVED. DO NOT REPRODUCE OR TRANSMIT THIS BOOK IN ANY FORM OR BY ANY MEANS, OH NO, NOT ELECTRONIC OR MECHANICAL, AND THAT INCLUDES RECORDING, PHOTO-COPYING, OR ANY INFORMATION STORAGE AND RETRIEVAL SYSTEM (AMAZING THINGS, NO?) WITHOUT PERMISSION FROM THE PUBLISHER (AMIABLE FELLOW).

PRINTING: FIRST PUBLISHED IN THE UNITED STATES OF AMERICA IN 1971 BY THE WALKER PUBLISHING COMPANY, INC.

PUBLISHED SIMULTANEOUSLY IN CANADA BY FITZHENRY & WHITESIDE, LIMITED, TORONTO.

PRINTED IN THE UNITED STATES OF A AMERICA BY AN ODD PROCESS.

COPYRIGHT: 1972 © BY **JAN ADKINS**
(THAT SLY DEVIL)

TH 481
.A33
PB
AUG 4 1983
SOUTH BOSTON BRANCH

PUSHPIN & ASSOC.
PURLIN RESIDENCE

DEDICATION

I DEDICATE THIS BOOK TO
TWO BEAUTIFUL GIRLS I KNOW:
MY SPECIAL WIFE DEBO, AND
MY SPARKLING, TWO-TOOTHED
DAUGHTER SALLY.

THIS IS CHARLIE AND ROSIE PURLIN, THEY LIVE HERE WITH SAM AND SALLY, MARCO THE GREAT DANE, FERDINAND AND ISABELLA (THEY LIVE IN THE CHANDELIER), AND AN OWL NAMED RALPH. YOU CAN SEE THAT THINGS HAVE GOTTEN A LITTLE CROWDED.

When Rosie's geranium fell into Charlie's pot of stew, they decided that they needed more space, a new home. They looked through stacks of newspapers, magazines and books for a house that was just right for the Purlin family, but none of the houses or apartments seemed to fit. They decided to have a house built for them, perfect for the Purlins.

PUSHPIN & ASSOC.
PURLIN RESIDENCE
THE LAST STRAW

6

PUSHPIN & ASSOC.
PURLIN RESIDENCE
A MORTGAGE

Houses are not paid for in the same way hot dogs are: buying a hot dog, you tell the hot dog man what you want on it, and he makes a hot dog with mustard and onions or catsup and relish, gives it to you, and you give him cash money, sometimes he gives you back change. Hardly anyone has enough money in their pockets or in their banks to pay for a house, which may cost more than Charlie makes in a whole year. Charlie and Rosie will borrow money from a bank to pay for having the house built now, and they will pay back part of the money each month for several years. They must pay back all the money they borrowed, and they must pay the bank for allowing them to use its money. This arrangement is called a <u>MORTGAGE</u>. With their banker's help, Charlie and Rosie figure out how much money they can afford to spend on the Purlin hous

After many weekends of driving from one place to another, they find a place to build their house, a grassy slope with trees. The piece of land a house is built on is called a SITE.

Many of the houses Charlie and Rosie have admired were designed by Alexander Pushpin and Associates. They are architects. Here is Mr. Pushpin and three of his associates, whom he has asked to help him design the Purlin home.

Charlie and Rosie talk with Mr. Pushpin and his associates many times, answering many questions about the way they think houses should be, about the way they live, so that the architects can design a house that helps them live and suits their needs. Rosie tells Mr. Pushpin that she would like to bring her groceries from the car directly into the kitchen, and you can see that he plans to have the kitchen beside the carport (and next to the diningroom, too).

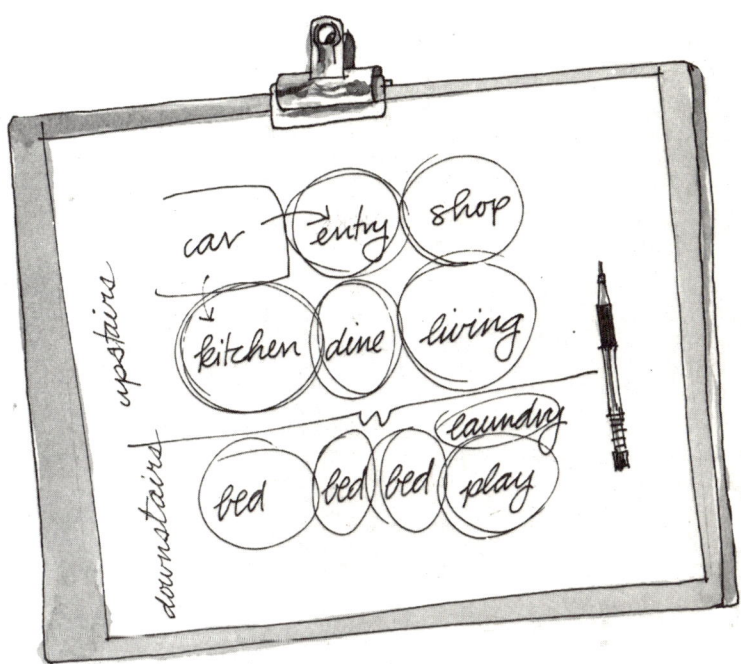

10 PUSHPIN & ASSOC.
PURLIN RESIDENCE
PLANS

A PEANUT — 5/8" × 1½"

AN APPLE PIE — 12" × 12"

A SANDBOX — 4'-0" × 4'-0"

If an architect had to talk to each workman every day, explaining just where to nail up each board and where to place every concrete block, then he would wear out his voice and not even a small house like the Purlin's would be finished. The architect talks to the workmen in a picture language that shows them how the house should be built, with measurements and details. He draws three kinds of pictures: ① PLANS, pictures of how things should be from above; ② ELEVATIONS, pictures of how things should be from the sides; ③ SECTIONS, cutaway pictures of how things work inside. The pictures of measurements are thin lines with cross-marks and dots, saying "The distance from this dot to the next is five feet and six inches (written → 5'-6"), the distance from that dot to the next is nine inches."

| 5'-6" | 9" |

HOW THINGS SHOULD BE FROM ABOVE, **PLANS**

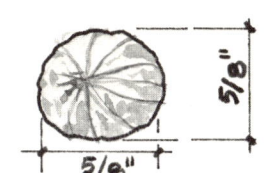

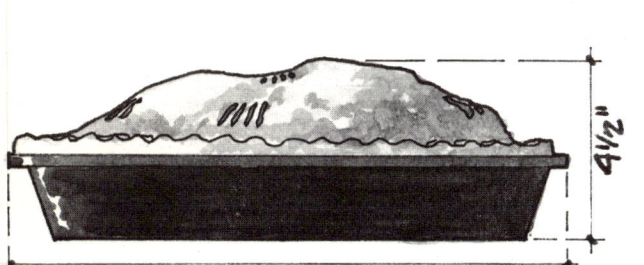
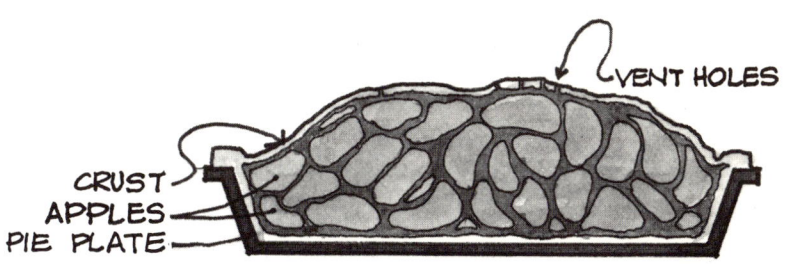

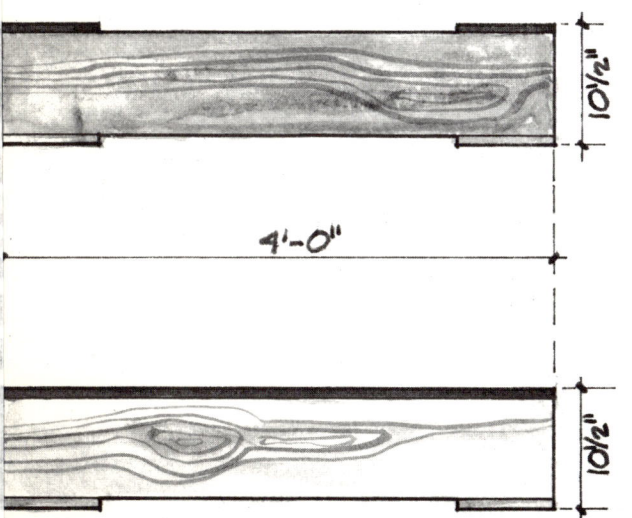
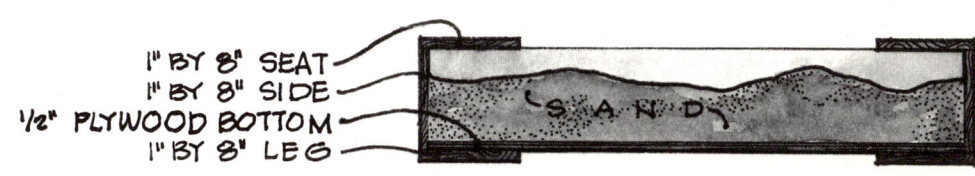

PUSHPIN & ASSOC.
PURLIN RESIDENCE
ELEVATIONS & SECTIONS

ELEVATIONS, HOW THINGS SHOULD BE FROM THE SIDES / HOW THINGS WORK INSIDE, SECTIONS

'11

To understand the plans of a house, imagine yourself from above, how would you look? Imagine yourself walking past Marco sleeping on the lawn and over to the sliding glass door, through the doorway and into the play area with the washer and dryer at the back wall. You could turn left and walk down the hall with the big windows on the outside wall, past the doors to Sam's room, Sally's room, and Charlie's and Rosie's bedroom, right to the stairs. If you walked up the stairs, you would be on the other page....

In the kitchen, facing the door to the carport. In the kitchen, you could walk to the right or left of the stove and be in the dining area. You could open the sliding glass door and walk out onto the sundeck, and if it was too sunny, walk under the roof and sit down beside Charlie, who may be asleep. If he were asleep, you could go back inside, through the living room, and past the coat closet into the entry area. The lavatory is there, and the door to the workshop. You could walk out the front door and into the driveway. If you turned around and looked at the front of the house, you would see an elevation, or a picture of how the house looked from that side, just as on sheet 14.

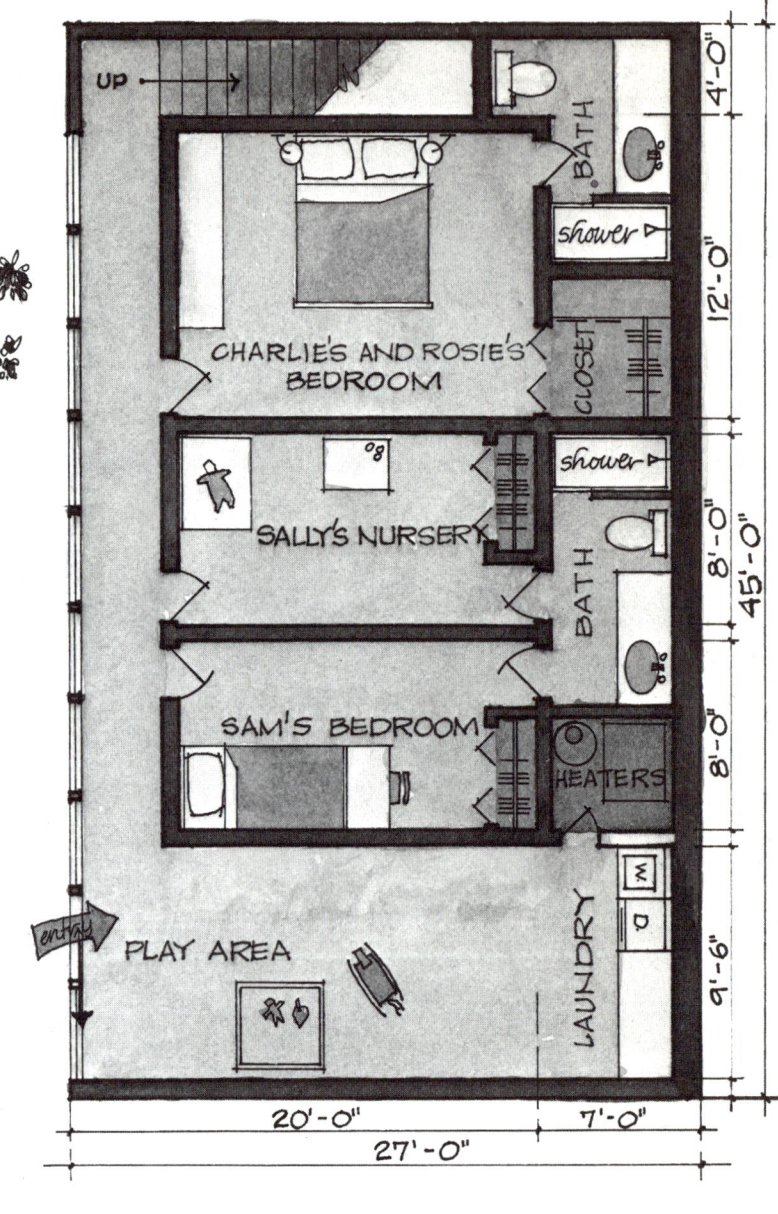

LOWER LEVEL   1/8" = 1'-0"

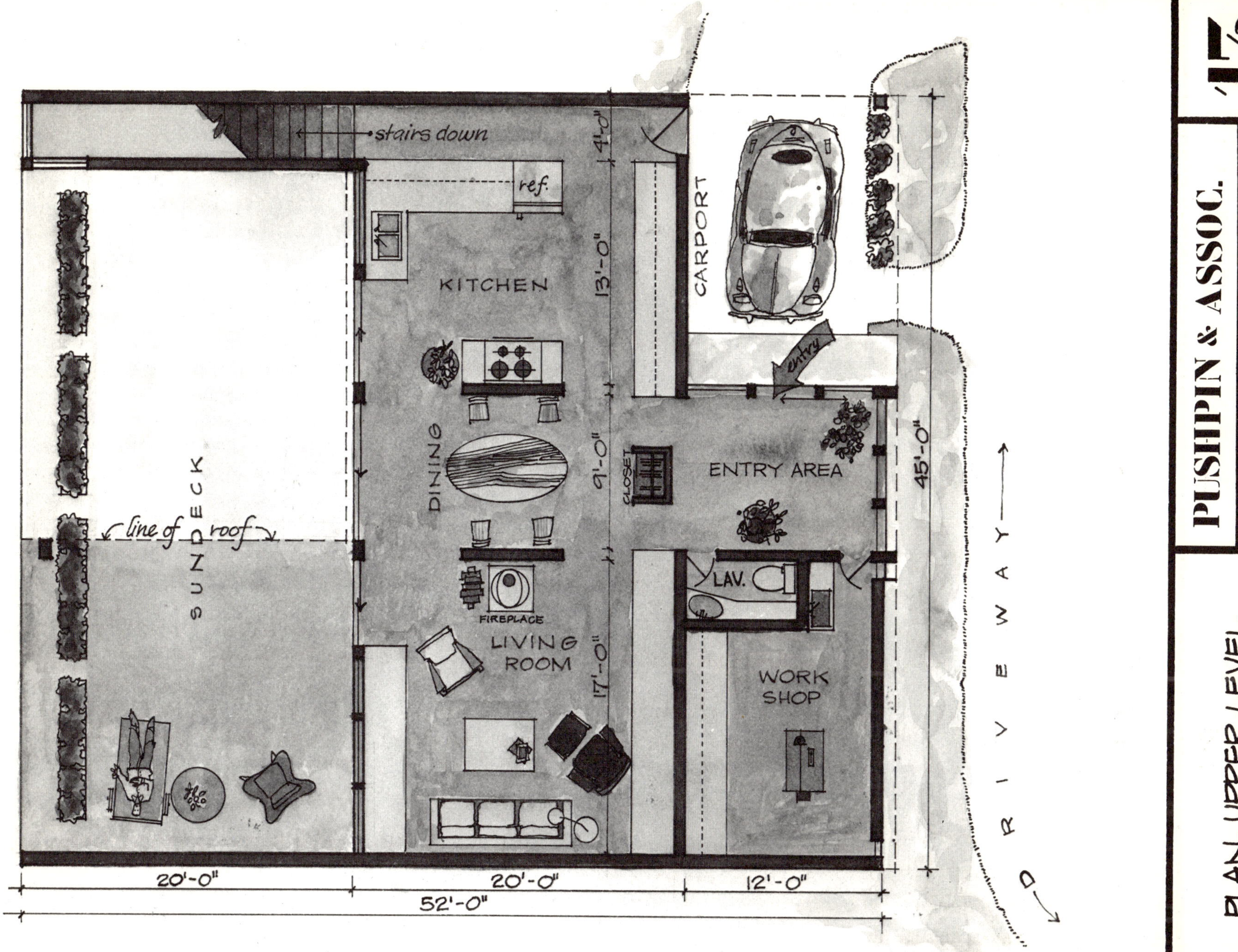

UPPER LEVEL   1/8" = 1'-0"

14

PUSHPIN & ASSOC.
PURLIN RESIDENCE
ELEVATIONS

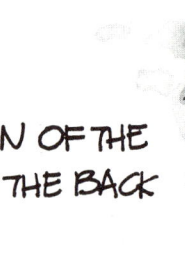

AN ELEVATION OF THE FRONT; FROM THE DRIVEWAY.

AN ELEVATION OF THE REAR; FROM THE BACK YARD.

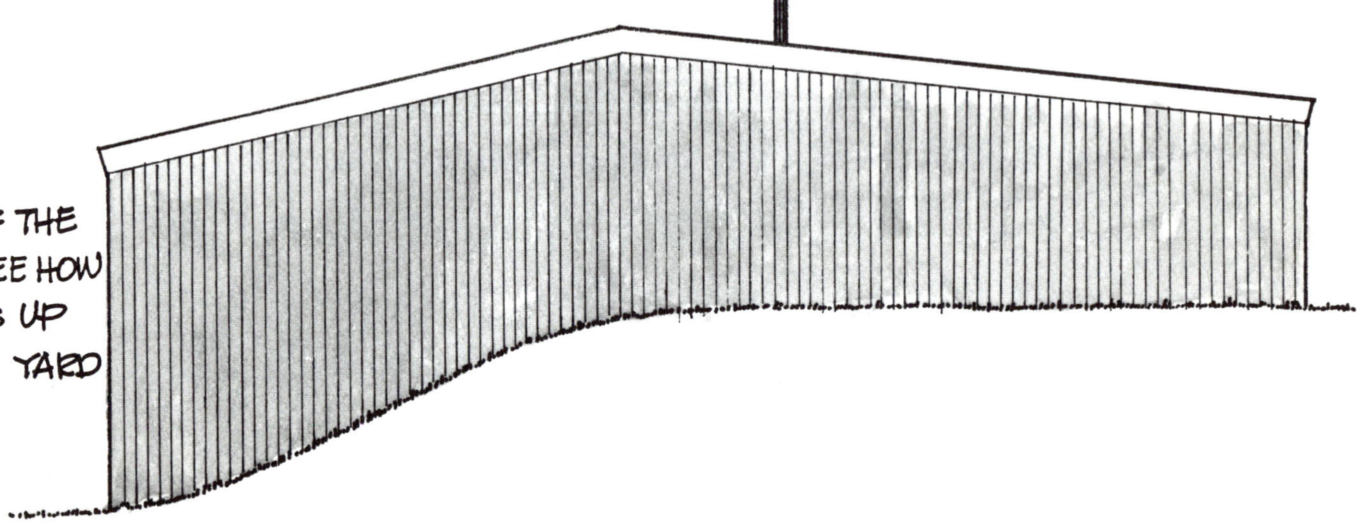

AN ELEVATION OF THE SIDE; YOU CAN SEE HOW THE SITE SLOPES UP FROM THE BACK YARD TO THE FRONT.

This section shows how the house would look if you could cut it across the kitchen, open it up, and look inside: you could see the kitchen cabinets (Rosie and Sam are in the kitchen), the sundeck outside, the bedroom on the lower level with its shower, and Marco is still asleep outside.

PUSHPIN & ASSOC.
PURLIN RESIDENCE
SECTION

16

PUSHPIN & ASSOC.
PURLIN RESIDENCE

THE CONTRACTOR

Charlie and Rosie like the design for the house. They ask a <u>CONTRACTOR</u> (the man whose company will actually build the house) to begin. Here is the contractor looking at the plans, figuring what he must order — how much lumber, cement, how many shingles and nails. A house is a complicated thing.

Finally, the house is begun! THE EXCAVATOR digs out the hillside to make space for the lower level. He digs between stakes placed very accurately by the SURVEYOR, who is still laying out the driveway. The excavator has protected the tree trunks from injury by tying boards around them.

PUSHPIN & ASSOC. '17

PURLIN RESIDENCE

EXCAVATION

'17

A HOUSE NEEDS A <u>FOUNDATION</u>: IT IS THE PLATFORM ON WHICH THE HOUSE MUST BE BUILT, BECAUSE THE EARTH IS TOO SOFT — PARTS OF THE HOUSE MIGHT SINK INTO LOOSE DIRT. IT IS EASY TO PUSH A PIN INTO AN ORANGE, BUT MUCH HARDER TO PUSH A PENCIL ERASER IN, BECAUSE THE ERASER IS BROADER AND PUSHES ON MORE OF THE ORANGE. IN THE SAME WAY, A THIN WALL MIGHT BE PUSHED INTO THE EARTH BY THE GREAT WEIGHT OF THE HOUSE, BUT WILL NOT BE PUSHED IN WITH A BROAD BASE OF CONCRETE BENEATH IT. THE FOUNDATION MEN DIG TRENCHES WHERE THE WALLS WILL MEET THE GROUND AND FILL THEM WITH LIQUID CEMENT. THEY SMOOTH THE SURFACE, AND WHEN THE CONCRETE HARDENS IN A FEW DAYS, IT IS READY TO SUPPORT THE WALLS.

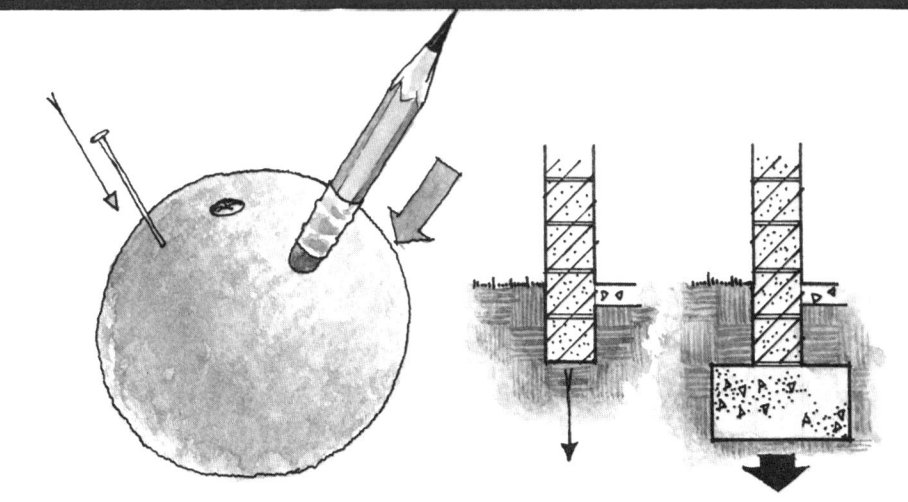

A CEMENT WORKER'S TOOLS ARE SIMPLE: A SHOVEL FOR TRENCHING, BOOTS FOR SLOSHING THROUGH THE CONCRETE.

The walls of the lower level must hold back the weight of the moist earth. Concrete block is strong and is not rotted or weakened when it is kept constantly moist, as wood is. Groundhogs do not chew through concrete block, either.

The masons place one layer of blocks on another, seating them firmly level in a bed of wet cement, called _mortar_. The mortar is handled with a trowel. The level and string are used to check the straightness of the layers (or _courses_) of block.

20

PUSHPIN & ASSOC.
PURLIN RESIDENCE
FRAMING AND SHEATHING

Now come the wooden walls. You can begin to see the shape of the house as <u>framing carpenters</u> nail up the boards that give the walls their strength. The boards are mostly <u>two by fours</u> (written "2×4's"). About two inches thick and four inches wide, they can be any length up to sixteen feet. Some wider boards are used: two by sixes (2×6's) may be used as <u>rafters</u> to hold the roof up; two by eights (2×8's) may be under the floor as <u>joists</u> to hold up the floor, or may be nailed with hard nails to the top of the concrete walls to give the framers wood to sink nails in. Plywood <u>sheathing</u> is nailed with twist nails to the framing, and the wall is begun.

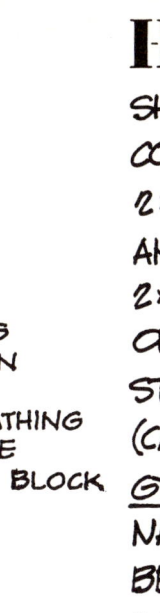

GYPSUM BOARD
EBOARD
1/2" WOOD
2x4 STUD
SIDING
SHEATHING
INSULATION
2x4
FLOOR SHEATHING
2x8 PLATE
CONCRETE BLOCK

HERE IS A SECTION (A CUTAWAY PICTURE OF HOW THINGS SHOULD LOOK INSIDE) OF THE WALL. YOU CAN SEE THE CONCRETE BLOCK COMING OUT OF THE GROUND, AND THE 2x8 <u>PLATE</u> ON IT. TO THE PLATE IS NAILED FLOORING, AND A 2x4 IS LAID FLAT ALONG THE EDGE. THE VERTICAL 2x4'S (CALLED <u>STUDS</u>) ARE NAILED INTO THE FLAT 2x4. ON THE OUTSIDE, PLYWOOD SHEATHING IS NAILED TO THE STUDS AND VERTICAL BOARDS TO FINISH THE OUTSIDE (CALLED <u>SIDING</u>) ARE NAILED TO IT. ON THE INSIDE, 1/2" <u>GYPSUM BOARD</u> — A WHITE, SMOOTH SHEET — IS CAREFULLY NAILED AFTER <u>INSULATION</u> IS PLACED IN THE SPACES BETWEEN STUDS. (THE GYPSUM BOARD WORKERS AND INSULATORS ARE ON SHEET 25.) THIS KIND OF WALL IS CALLED A <u>STUD WALL</u>.

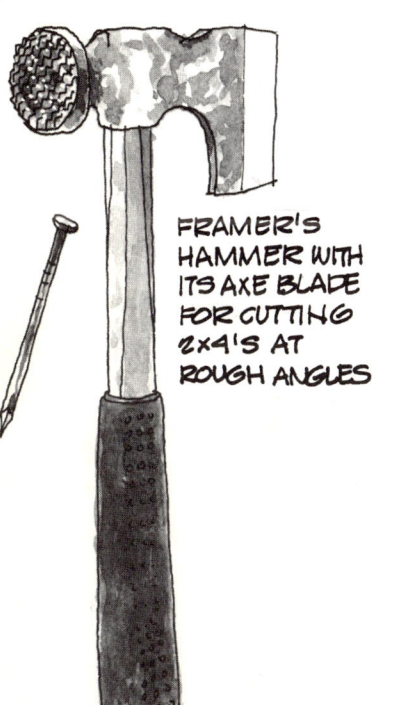

FRAMER'S HAMMER WITH ITS AXE BLADE FOR CUTTING 2x4'S AT ROUGH ANGLES

HAMMER AND TWIST NAIL FOR SHEATHING

PUSHPIN & ASSOC.

PURLIN RESIDENCE

WALL EXPLANATION

21

It's time to make a roof over the Purlin house. Plywood is nailed to the 2×6 rafters, which are set at a slope to prevent water from rolling up under the overlapping shingles. Overlapping tarpaper is nailed under the shingles in case some disobedient water might find its way under an off-duty shingle. There is also insulation in the roof.

Some of the roofer's tools are: a hammer, short roofing nails, and a curved knife to cut shingles and tarpaper.

Before the stud walls are enclosed from both sides, the plumbing and electricity must be installed, since their pipes and wires are almost always inside walls and floors. The plumber is working on the drainpipe that will be attached to the sink in the lavatory located off the entry area on the upper level. If you look back to the plans on sheet 3, you can see where he is. Hot and cold water pipes come up for the sink, there, one cold water pipe for the toilet and its drain in the floor.

The electrician is running lines from the switch boxes, through holes he has bored in the studs, to the lights.

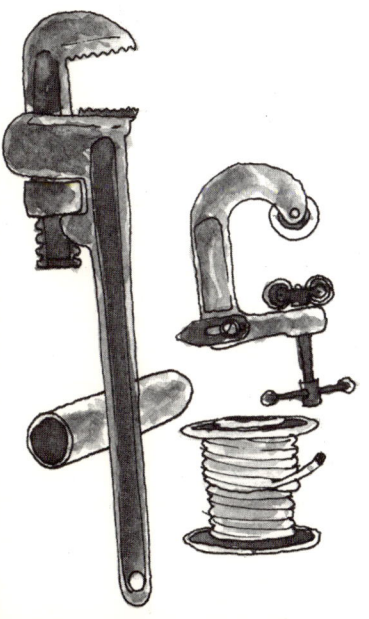

The plumber uses pipe of copper and steel and plastic, big wrenches, and wrench-like pipe cutters, rolls of solder, a blowtorch and many other tools. The electrician carries many of his tools in a belt-hung leather pouch: screwdriver, pliers, wire-stripper, black plastic electrical tape.

24

PUSHPIN & ASSOC.
PURLIN RESIDENCE
GLAZING & HEATING

From the furnace on the lower level, the heating man installs ducts, box-like tubes made of sheet-metal, running through walls and floors to each room. The ducts will carry warm air in winter, cool air in summer. You can see two ducts with their covers beside them, coming out of the floor in the kitchen. One comes up beneath the sink (can you see the plumbing for the sink?). Glazers install windows, as these two glazers are placing the window that Rosie will look through as she stands at the sink. One of the sliding glass doors is leaning in its opening with masking tape stuck on its plate glass so that workmen won't try to walk or throw tools through it.

Some of the sheet-metal worker's tools: a drill to make holes in the metal, special short screws, a screwdriver, and large shears.

After the insulator staples his rolls of fiberglass insulation into the spaces between rafters and studs, the gypsum board workers can cover the wiring, plumbing, ductwork, and studs with a smooth surface. First, the sheets of gypsum board are nailed to the studs with thin nails, then tape is fixed over the seams between sheets. Finally, the tape and nail-heads are spackled over (covered smoothly with a fine, white paste).

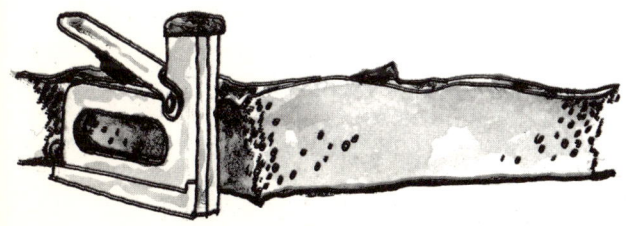

FOIL-BACKED FIBERGLASS INSULATION AND STAPLE GUN

THIN GYPSUM-BOARD NAILS, TAPE, A TUB OF SPACKLING PASTE AND A SPACKLING KNIFE.

26

PUSHPIN & ASSOC.
PURLIN RESIDENCE

FINISH CARPENTRY

The finish carpenter carefully builds the cabinets and counters and closets in kitchen and bathrooms. Here he is working at the kitchen cabinets while the refrigerator is being moved into place. Some of his tools are: a mitre saw and mitre box for cutting angles, headless finishing nails and a nail set to sink them, chisel for cutting grooves.

The painter arrives with his cans, ladders, and brushes, and leaves when the house has its coat of many colors. The tilers and carpeters come, and when they go the floors have colors and textures. Men come with appliances, women come with drapes, they go away and leave the house more beautiful and more complete. The moving men come, they carry and sweat, their truck rolls away and the house is furnished. Then the house is complete, it is finished, right? No.

PUSHPIN & ASSOC.
PURLIN RESIDENCE
PAINTING, MISC.

28 PUSHPIN & ASSOC. — PURLIN RESIDENCE — FINISHED HOUSE

"A house is most of all the people in it. The 2×4's, the windows, the shingles, the pipes and wiring and ducts, the cabinets and gypsum board mean nothing at all without Rosie and Charlie and Sally and Sam living in the house, laughing in it, eating and working and crying and sleeping in it. Alexander Pushpin and his associates designed it just for that, the framers and plumbers and painters and all the workmen worked so that it could happen. The Purlin family make the Purlin house."

A house is a place to live in.

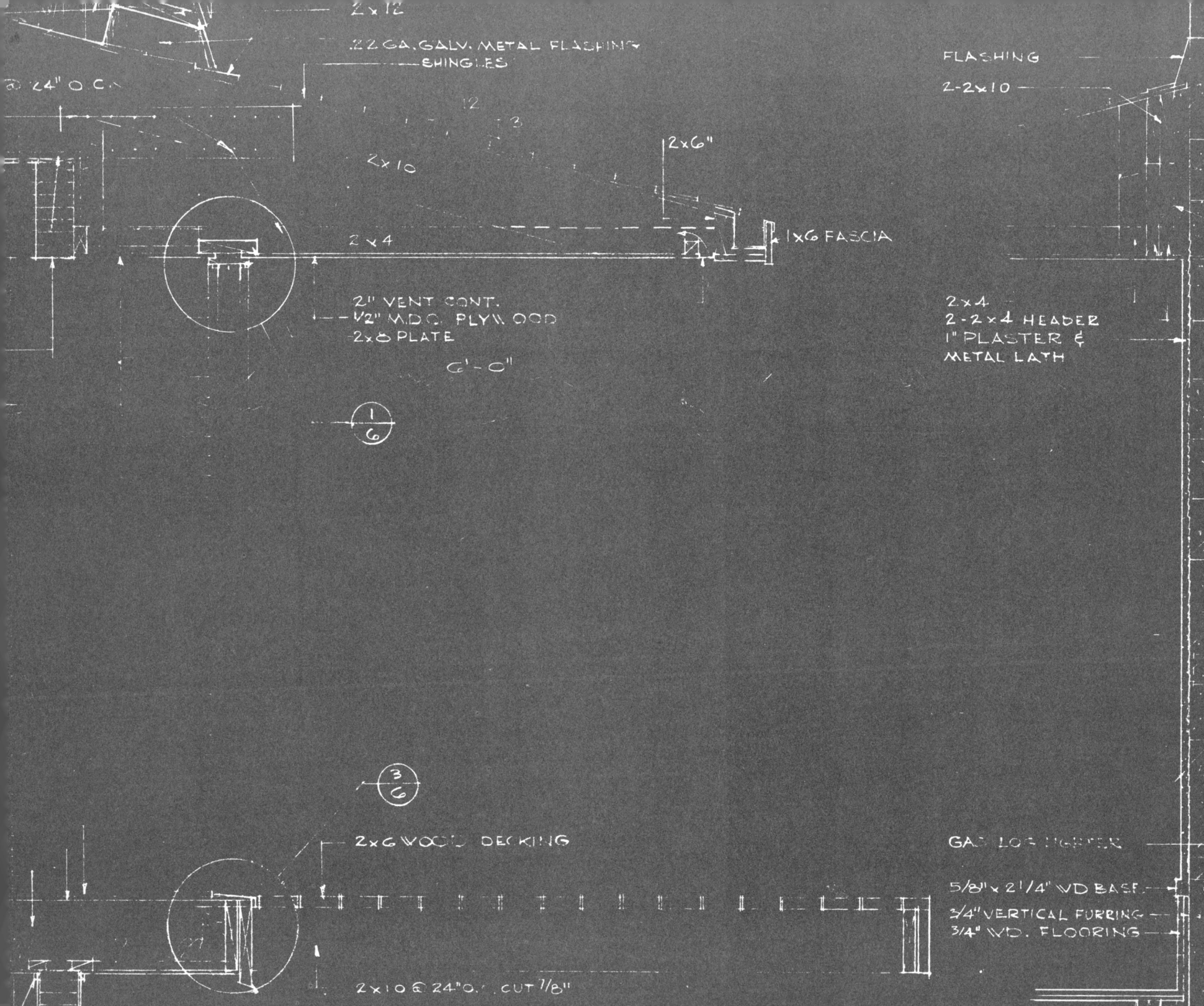

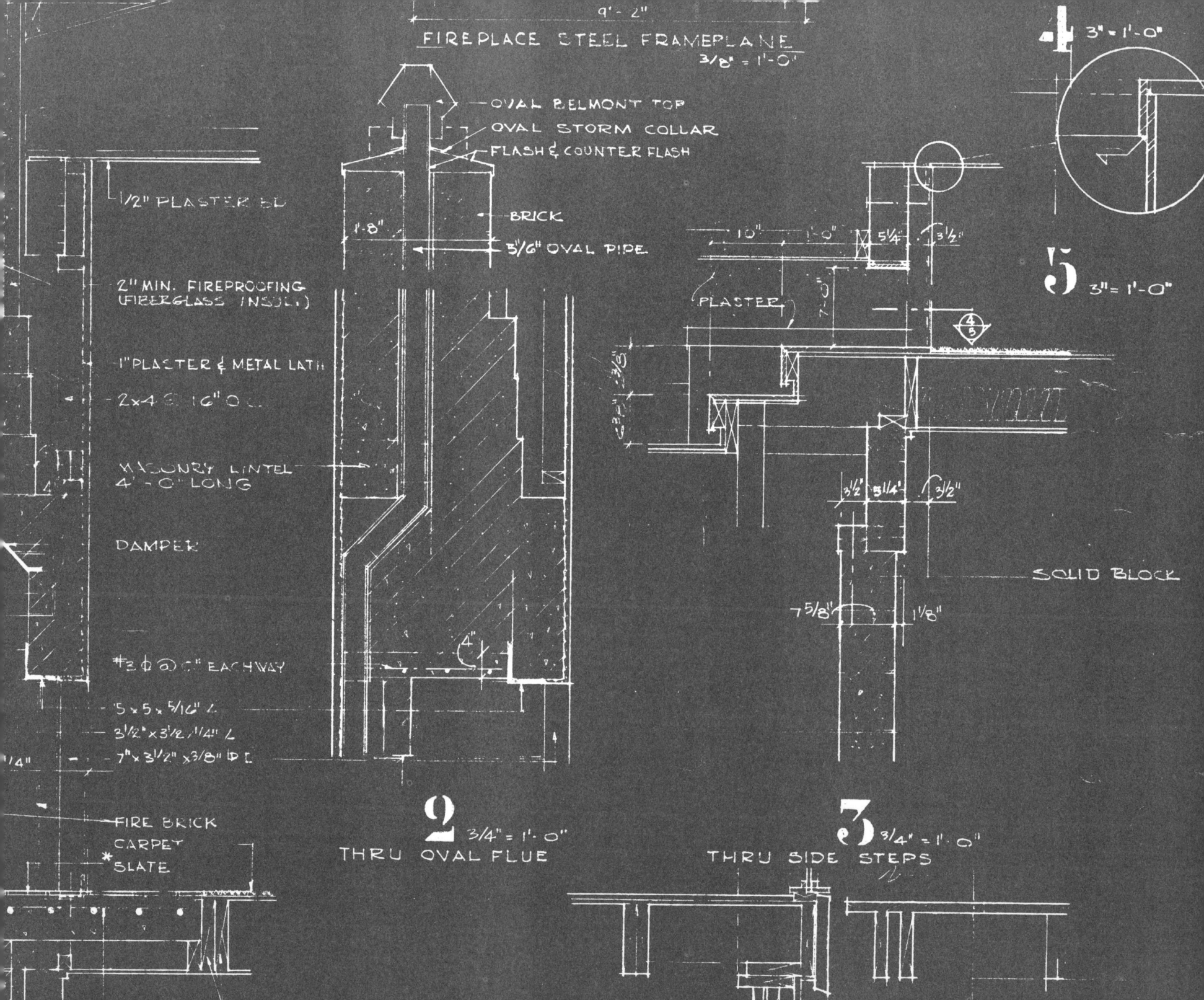

31

WITHDRAWN FOR DISCARD